YOUR KNOWLEDGE HAS VALUE

A Deep Learning Based Spontaneous Retail Product Identification

Upesh Patel
Sachi Joshi

Bibliographic information published by the German National Library:

The German National Library lists this publication in the National Bibliography; detailed bibliographic data are available on the Internet at http://dnb.dnb.de.

ISBN: 9783346967350
This book is also available as an ebook.

© GRIN Publishing GmbH
Trappentreustraße 1
80339 München

Print and binding: Books on Demand GmbH, Norderstedt, Germany
Printed on acid-free paper from responsible sources.

The present work has been carefully prepared. Nevertheless, authors and publishers do not incur liability for the correctness of information, notes, links and advice as well as any printing errors.

GRIN web shop: https://www.grin.com/document/1416457

A Deep Learning Based Spontaneous Retail Product Identification

ABSTRACT

The concept of self-service retail store has been successfully adopted around the world since its inception in 1916 United States of America. People carry their required retail products in a cart, hand-basket and make their purchase by standing in the queue to make payment. With advancements in electronics and computer sciences, this project aims to ease the "traditional purchase experience" at the same time maintaining the conventional "Hold-Observe-Purchase" experience by attempting to automate the billing procedure. Using deep learning algorithms and Image processing principles, the product images are recognized and its pertaining information is used to generate the transactional ledger as the products are added. This phase of the project aims at training our model to recognize custom images of Indian Retail products more specifically "Indian Consumable Retail products". Furthermore, the trained model is deployed on a **"Single Board Computer (SBC)"** such as **"Raspberry Pi 4"** to recognize the product images by taking its picture **with the Raspberry Pi camera attached to the SBC** and running the image through the trained model to identify it and generate the transaction ledger.

Objective

- Primary objective to develop this project, was to eliminate the need of long payment queues especially in weekends in retail stores by automating the payment procedure.

- Implementing a complex principle of image recognition to promote **"Digital payment revolution in India under atmanirbhar bharat"** as predicted results are used to generate the transactional ledger.

- To learn and create a custom image data set of the retail products using data augmentation and image processing principles which is comprised of internet search results and photos captured by smart phone.

- To deploy a pre-trained image recognition algorithm (trained on Laptop computer) on a SBC such as raspberry pi attached with a camera which can capture image and can conveniently execute the pre trained model bypassing the need of advanced computation power.

Flow Chart

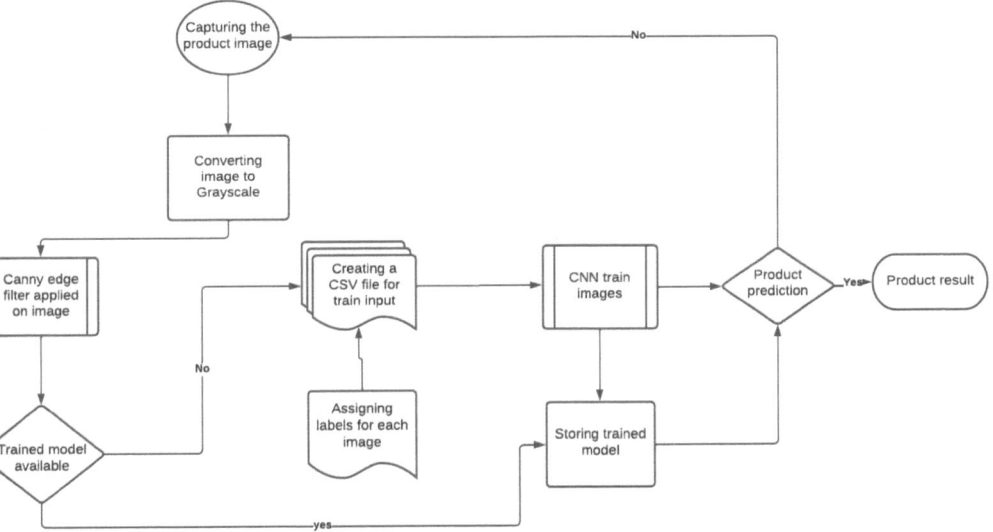

Figure1: Software implementation

1.1 Deep Learning

❖ Deep Learning is a subfield of **Machine Learning** which specifically deals with implementing algorithms that mimic the structure as well as function of **neurons of human brain [1].**

❖ Deep Learning is primarily a **supervised learning** technique, which maps inputs to its corresponding outputs based on the correct solution given for the corresponding input. The so called **training model** is trained with examples associated with the accurate output as well as the desired accurate output.

❖ All the Training algorithms are based on the **biological Neuron.** The structure of neuron is given as below:

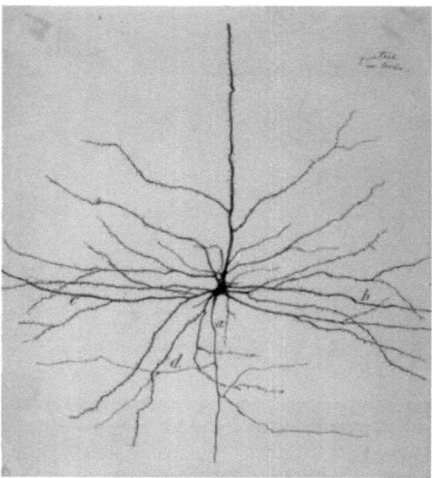

Figure 1.1 A typical Neuron

❖ As per the Fig 1.1, the neuron is primarily composed of 3 parts:

1. **Dendrites:** They serve as multiple inputs from other neurons, depicted in this image as the branches emanating from the center.
2. **Central body:** The **primary computation unit** which processes our neural information and its amalgamation makes up the mind.
3. **Axon:** The vertical from the top of the image emerging as a branch from the central body serves as the **output of the computation** and as **one of the input of the next neuron in the process [2].**

1.2 Perceptron

❖ Primary example of deep learning algorithm that resembles the structure and function of a neuron is **Perceptron.**

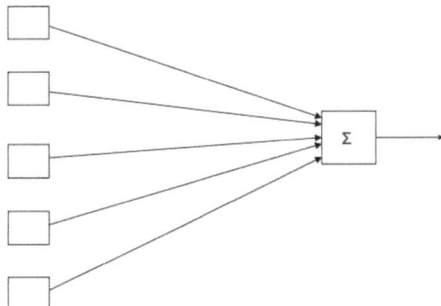

Figure 1.2 Structure of Neurons

❖ Echoing the structure of Neurons, the perceptron has multiple inputs (imitating dendrites) which depends upon the nature of data which is then fed to the computation unit:

1. **Input:** where the features are taken in as input. **Denoted by X**

2. **Weight:** Weights are scalar values that are multiplied with the in input values (**denoted by W**) which essentially help in driving the input values closer to the accurate output; the correct values of **Weight** determines the accuracy of the perceptron. **Bias:** It is an additional weight added to the perceptron. Denoted by b.

❖ The above mentioned terms are denoted as "Parameters of a Neural Network".

❖ The perceptron is denoted as Φ, specifically as F(Φ).

❖ With these parameters the perceptron computes the following function:

$$f_\Phi(\mathbf{x}) = \begin{cases} 1 & \text{if } b + \sum_{i=1}^{l} x_i w_i > 0 \\ 0 & \text{otherwise} \end{cases}$$

Figure 1.3 Function

❖ Here the above function implements a binary classification, where it takes pixel values as input for an image for example and trains the model based on the pixel values.

❖ The algorithm works by iterating over the training set several times **adjusting the parameters several times to increase the number of accurately identified inputs.**

❖ If the training model gets through the data set without modifying the parameters, then it can be said that the data set is correct and the iterations can be limited. But in real life applications it is not possible as a result, as long as considerable accurate values are not obtained the algorithm must iterate through the data set and continuously update and modify the parameters[3-5].

❖ **Method to modify/update the parameters to drive towards accurate prediction values:**

      1. set b and all of the **w**'s to 0.

      2. for N iterations, or until the weights do not change

          (a) for each training example $\mathbf{x}^k$ with answer a^k

              i. if $a^k - f(\mathbf{x}^k) = 0$ continue

              ii. else for all weights w_i, $\Delta w_i = (a^k - f(\mathbf{x}^k))x_i$

Figure 1.4 Function

❖ Here in Fig 1.4, the perceptron function F(x) is constantly subtracted from the accurate output i.e. (pixel value of the output) to check if the predicted value is closer to the actual one. If the result is 0 or a value near to it then the perceptron has accurately predicted the value.

❖ But if the value is greater than 0 or different then the **weights corresponding to the particular input in that iteration must be updated by the pixel value or the input value.**

1.3 Convolutional Neural Networks (CNN):

Perceptron as observed earlier, mimic biological neuron and how it utilizes input data and parameters to predict accurate results, now a more complex and efficient algorithm that is based on the structure and function of perceptrons are **Convolutional Neural Networks(CNN).**

❖ CNN have input layer and an output layer just like perceptron. It also has multiple hidden layers that helps in prediction of accurate results, these layers help in extracting necessary information which represent the data and are **primary cornerstone that enable the algorithm to differentiate different inputs.**

1.3.1 Convolutional Neural Network Layers:

❖ **Input Layer:** Through this layer, the input is fed to the algorithm. The number of neurons in the layer are determined by the number of features a data has for example a training image for image recognition is of dimension 100x100 then total number of neurons in this layer are 10000.

❖ **Output Layer:** The number of neurons in this layer depends upon the purpose of the algorithm. If the algorithm is trained on some data to classify in terms of '**1**' or '**0**' then the number of neuron in this layer is only 1 as it is binary classification. Now if the problem is of multi class classification then the number of neurons in the output layer depends upon the number of different classes the input data belongs to. This layer is also known as **fully connected layer,** this layer receives an input vector from hidden layers and gives out the output vector of **probability of each class. Each element of the output vector indicates the probability for the input image to belong to a class.** To calculate the probabilities, the fully-connected layer, therefore, multiplies each input element by weight, makes the sum, and then applies an activation function i.e. **softmax.**

❖ **The Hidden layers:**

- **Convolution Layer:** The purpose of this layer is to detect the presence of features of data for example in image (pixel values) i.e edges. This is achieved by convolution filter, it is a matrix of size 3x3 which performs the convolution product on the pixel values with the values of matrix and slides from left to right for each row in the image matrix. This operation highlights important features of image and more importantly scales down the data matrix with just highlighted important features (**feature map**). So, the higher the value of feature, the more corresponding place in the image resembles the feature matrix.

- **Pooling Layer:** This kind of layers is often placed between convolution layers, it receives **feature map as input** from previous convolution layer and scales down the feature map to important features required using **pooling.** Pooling extracts higher feature values from the feature matrix by sliding a patch/filter from left to right for each row starting from top left of the feature map and creates a reduced matrix of **higher feature value thus it reduces the number of parameters and calculations in the network.**

- **ReLu correction layer:** The computation as seen earlier Fig 1.1.2 is known as **Linear Unit.** ReLU stands for **Rectified Linear Units represented as ReLu(X) = max(0,X)**which helps in reducing the mathematical computation as by replacing negative values with **0s. It acts as an activation function.** An activation function activates a neuron based on a threshold value where values greater than 0 are replaced with 1 and vice versa i.e when the output of a ReLu unit is 1 the corresponding neuron is activated and it's output is fed to the output layer which has **softmax(as it's activation function) in the case of multi class classification which returns the highest value output of that neuron among all the neurons representing classes in the output layer.**

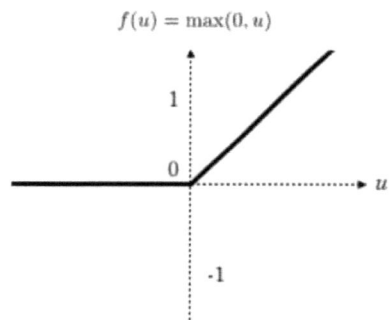

Figure 1.5 ReLU Representation

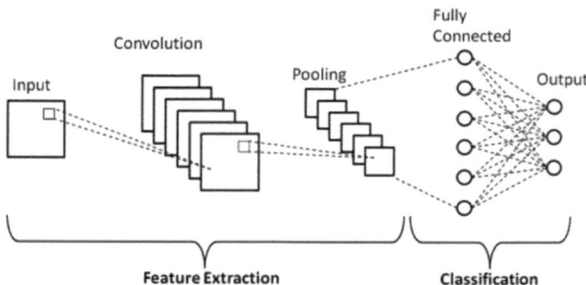

Figure 1.6 CNN Diagram

1.4   The Tools

➤ **OpenCV:** Open Computer Vision is a library mainly aimed at developing computer vision applications such as image object recognition, real time object recognition, image processing functionalities enable user to integrate it with machine learning algorithms.

➤ **Pandas:** Pandas is a python based open source data analysis tool which enables user to use different data structures to manipulate real time data such as numerical tabular data. In this project it enabled to convert image pixel values to comma separated value file.

➤ **Keras:** Keras is a open-source machine learning library aimed at providing interface for deep learning that is artificial neural network. It acts as an interface for the tensorflow library. It contains numerous neural network building tools such as adding new layers, activation functions, optimizers, etc.

➤ **Tensorflow:** Tensorflow is a free open-source machine learning library developed by google which supports developing deep learning applications across C++ and python. Tensorflow is the engine program for Keras previously discussed and powers keras to develop, deploy and train neural networks.

1.5   Creating the training data set

1.5.1   Importance of the dataset

1. Data plays pivotal role in the vast domain of Machine learning, almost every application of machine learning rely on data be it in the form of image, text, speech. Machine learning algorithms mine essential information from data sets for different purposes such as to gain insight from financial data to chart new investment and transactions, to recognize objects in real time and from images which has myriad applications in medical sciences, robotics, meteorological predictions, etc. The nature of data determines the direction in which any machine learning model can be applied. The importance of amount of data is extremely paramount because the accuracy of any machine learning algorithm depends on it. If the machine learning

model is not trained with sufficient amount of data, the predictions it makes will not be much accurate and hence unreliable.

2. Discussing the importance of data at a good length, one must be aware that in order to apply deep learning model to real life applications the data required is not completely ideal in nature. In this project "Retail Product Identification" the primary focus of the model used are **Indian retail products.** The primary requirement therefore was to create custom image dataset to train the model. There are 8 different consumable products on which the CNN is trained.

1.6   Images

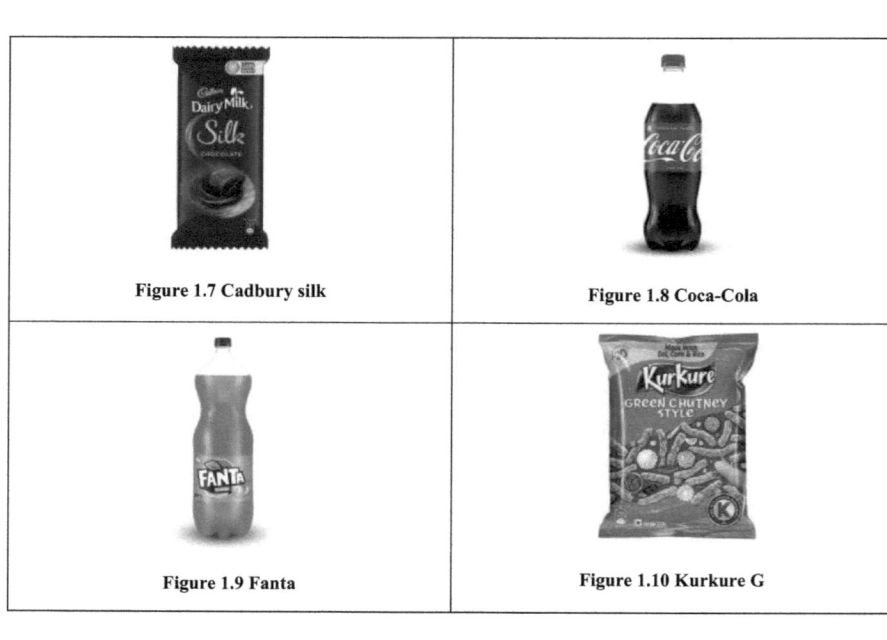

Figure 1.7 Cadbury silk	Figure 1.8 Coca-Cola
Figure 1.9 Fanta	Figure 1.10 Kurkure G

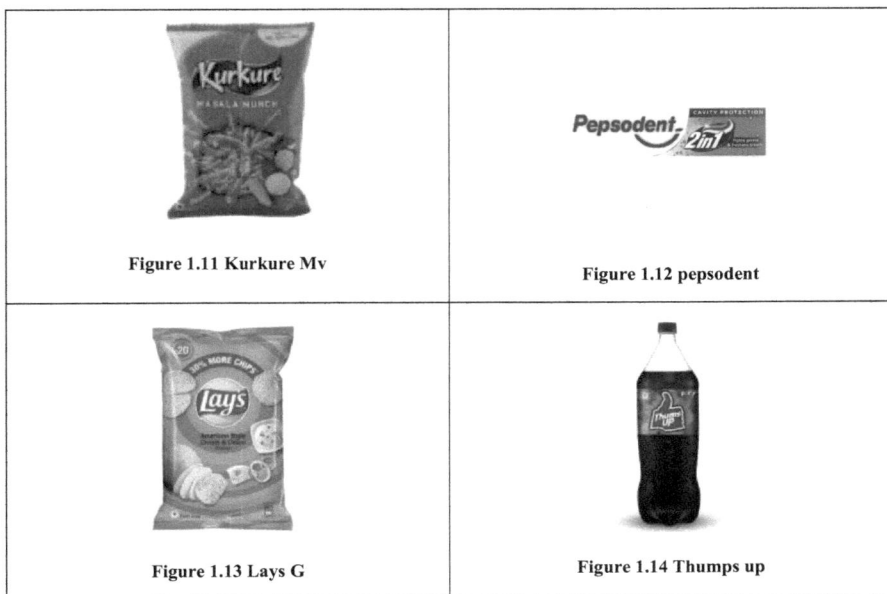

Figure 1.11 Kurkure Mv	**Figure 1.12 pepsodent**
Figure 1.13 Lays G	**Figure 1.14 Thumps up**

1.7   Data Augmentation

1. As per chapter 2, for applying deep learning principles in real life applications, the need for custom datasets is a necessity. As the importance of sufficient data required to train the model was discussed at a good length in previous chapter 2.

2. **Data Augmentation enables user to create multiple copies of an image with different orientation, angle, zoom.** This powerful tool enables user to create sufficient volume of data so that machine learning model can be trained properly. This tool is a part of **Keras library.**

```
[1]: import pandas as pd
     import numpy as np
     import cv2
     from keras.preprocessing.image import ImageDataGenerator
     import os

[3]: datagen = ImageDataGenerator(
             rotation_range=45,      #Random rotation between 0 and 45
             width_shift_range=0.2,  #% shift
             height_shift_range=0.2,
             shear_range=0.2,
             zoom_range=0.2,
             horizontal_flip=True,
             fill_mode='constant', cval=125)

[26]: #i = 0
      def Image_generator_Lays(path1,path2):
          i = 0
          for batch in datagen.flow_from_directory(directory=path1,
                               batch_size=10,
                               target_size=(100, 100),
                               color_mode="rgb",
                               save_to_dir=path2,
                               save_prefix='lay',
                               save_format='jpg'):
              i += 1
              if i > 199:
                  break
```

Figure 1.15 Data Augmentation

3. The method can be called using **Imagedatagenerator** which returns an object in user variable.

a) **Rotation_range-** Here the images generated using ImageDataGenerator have been tilted upto 45 degree angle.

b) **Width_shift** = The width is shifted in the range -1 to 1 with interval of 0.2

c) **Height_shift** = The height is shifted in the range -1 to 1 with interval of 0.2

d) **Sheer_range** = The interval defined for manipulating the angle at which image exists.

e) **zoom_range** = The interval defined for which the image is zoomed at different regions.

4. **For batch in datagen.flow_from_directory** enables to create augment images present in different folders in a common directory and store it in a unique directory as per the user. Also Image can be saved in different formats; color mode of the image can be defined and more importantly **dimensions of the image can be defined. Here iterative variable 'I' can be used to generate desired number of images.**

5. **Data Augmentation output**

11

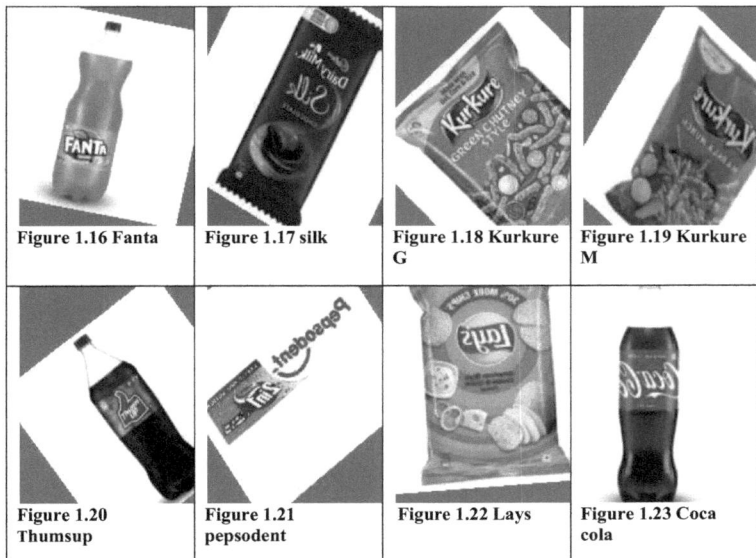

Figure 1.16 Fanta	Figure 1.17 silk	Figure 1.18 Kurkure G	Figure 1.19 Kurkure M
Figure 1.20 Thumsup	Figure 1.21 pepsodent	Figure 1.22 Lays	Figure 1.23 Coca cola

1.8 Canny Edge Detection

1. Deep learning algorithms are specifically used in computer vision based problems, where the data is mostly in the form of image or a video or real time video recording. So naturally the features of the image are going to be the pixel values that determine the results of the prediction. Also change in pixel values alter the entire prediction.

2. Primary features of the image are edges, texture, shape and size, but many times different objects having similar size and shape are often not recognized by the learning algorithm and as a result they are predicted inaccurately. This is a major problem recognized for Indian retail products, the amount of information present in an image of a single product is more than it's shape and size. In order to extract those pixel values, **canny edge detection filter is used which highlight the texture of images** thereby highlighting the information present in the image along with it's shape and size.

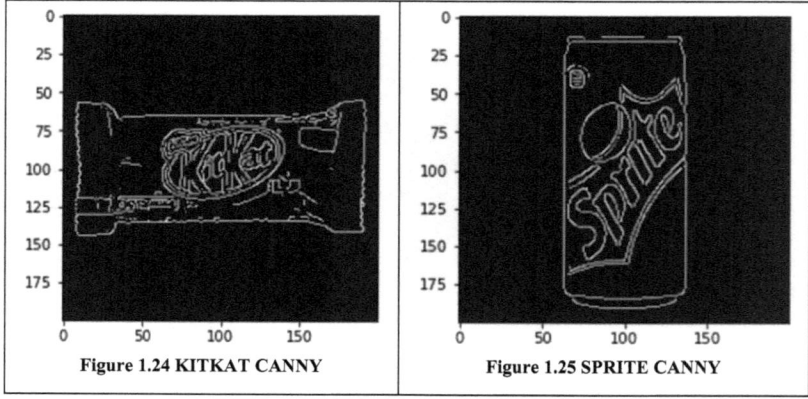

Figure 1.24 KITKAT CANNY | Figure 1.25 SPRITE CANNY

1.9   Data Extraction

1. Importing necessary libraries to read, modify images as per the requirement.

```python
import cv2 #opencv for reading images
from matplotlib import pyplot as plt #to view images if required
import os,glob #os, glob enable's user to explore folders
#and be manipulated as such
from os import listdir,makedirs#allows to take entire content of folder as input
from os.path import isfile,join
import pandas as pd# pandas provides Dataframe to store image pixels
```

Figure 1.26 Libraries

2. Now there are 8 different kind of Indian retail product more specifically consumables across 8 different folders in a directory. Also there are more than 1000 images per folder due to image augmentation to provide a sufficient training volume to the training model.

13

```
def image_features(path):
    data = []
    for image in os.listdir(path):
        img = cv2.imread(os.path.join(path,image),cv2.IMREAD_GRAYS
        dim = (100,100)
        img = cv2.resize(img,dim)
        img2 = img.reshape(-1)
        #print(len(img.shape))
        #applying edge detection filter as canny
        canny = cv2.Canny(img,100,100)
        canny1 = canny.reshape(-1)
        #im_resize=np.reshape(img,(40000,1))
        #canny = np.reshape(canny,(40000,1))
        data.append(img2)
        data.append(canny1)
    return data
```

Figure 1.27 Image features

a) Now the above method takes input as an image from desired folder, reads it as a grayscale image and stores it in a user variable. The image is resized to 100x100 to ease based on the computer and reshaped to a single dimension matrix.

b) **Img = cv2.imread(,cv2.IMREAD_GRAYSCALE)** reads images in grayscale that is single channel format.

c) **os.path.join(path,image)** essentially takes the iterative variable image and assigns it to every file present in the folder i.e the path, as the file and it's path is available it is easy to read images. This method enables the user to automatically pick images from given path.

d) **Cv2.resize()** takes an image as an argument and returns a resized image as per the given dimension value by the user.

e) **Cv2.Canny()** takes an image and it's dimensions as an argument and returns an edge detected result back, highlighting all the edges of the image for efficient training.

f) The canny filter image and the original image pixel values are stored in an array. The method returns the array.

3. Now after all pixel values of each image has been extracted and stored in an array, a combined data frame needs to be created for the pixel values of entire training volume comprised of thousands of images

14

```
def image_operations(image, name):
    traindata = []#holds all the pixel values
    #temp = pd.DataFrame() #temporarily holds all the image data
    traindata = image_features(image)
    temp = pd.DataFrame(traindata)
    temp['10000'] = name
    return temp
```

Figure 1.28 Image operations()

a) This function was conceived after many failed attempts, this method calls the earlier **image_features()** method which extracts image pixel values in an array and returns that array. This method uses that array to create a data frame. Also this function let's the user to assign a label to the particular image being added to the data frame as it's argument **name** (name of the image or assigned label) and the image itself.

b) **Traindata** holds the return value of the previously discussed method and uses it to create a dataframe.

c) **Pd.DataFrame()** takes an array as an input and uses it's values to create a Data frame a 2 dimensional data frame where the number of pixels serve as it's columns and the number of images are rows.

d) Now the dimensions of the image are 100x100 it means that there are 10000 pixel values so the column values of the data frame ranges from 0 to 9999 for that image. Now a label to recognize the image or the correct answer to that image must be added while it's data frame is created (**supervised learning**) so a new column of label i.e column number 10000 is added and it's label is assigned. Later these columsn can be dropped as labels for the training model but that part will be covered in detail in further chapters. Data frame is returned.

4. Now implementing above methods:

```
: train_data = pd.DataFrame()

: cadbury = r'C:\Users\91989\Documents\1FINAL PROJECT\train\grayscale\Train\cadbury_silk'

: cadbury_silk=image_operations(cadbury,0)

: cadbury_silk
```

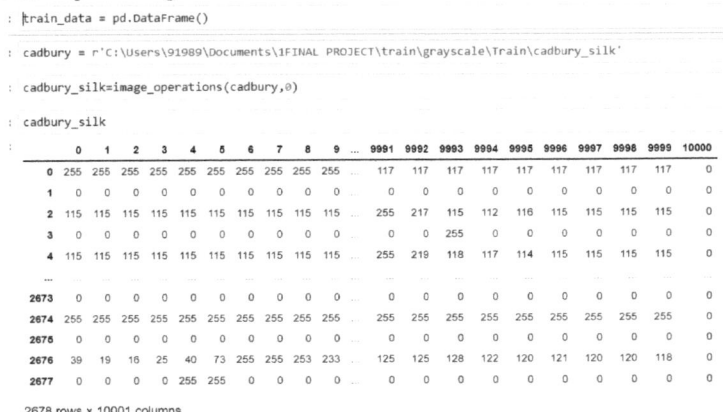

	0	1	2	3	4	5	6	7	8	9	...	9991	9992	9993	9994	9995	9996	9997	9998	9999	10000
0	255	255	255	255	255	255	255	255	255	255	...	117	117	117	117	117	117	117	117	117	0
1	0	0	0	0	0	0	0	0	0	0	...	0	0	0	0	0	0	0	0	0	0
2	115	115	115	115	115	115	115	115	115	115	...	255	217	115	112	116	115	115	115	115	0
3	0	0	0	0	0	0	0	0	0	0	...	0	0	255	0	0	0	0	0	0	0
4	115	115	115	115	115	115	115	115	115	115	...	255	219	118	117	114	115	115	115	115	0
...																					
2673	0	0	0	0	0	0	0	0	0	0	...	0	0	0	0	0	0	0	0	0	0
2674	255	255	255	255	255	255	255	255	255	255	...	255	255	255	255	255	255	255	255	255	0
2675	0	0	0	0	0	0	0	0	0	0	...	0	0	0	0	0	0	0	0	0	0
2676	39	19	16	25	40	73	255	255	253	233	...	125	125	128	122	120	121	120	120	118	0
2677	0	0	0	0	255	255	0	0	0	0	...	0	0	0	0	0	0	0	0	0	0

2678 rows × 10001 columns

Figure 1.29 Cadbury silk data frame

a) Here the pixel values of 2678 cadbury image is loaded into the dataframe along with it's label '**0**'.

b) This step continues for all the images of all classes.

5. The final data frame created for all pixel values of each product are as follows:

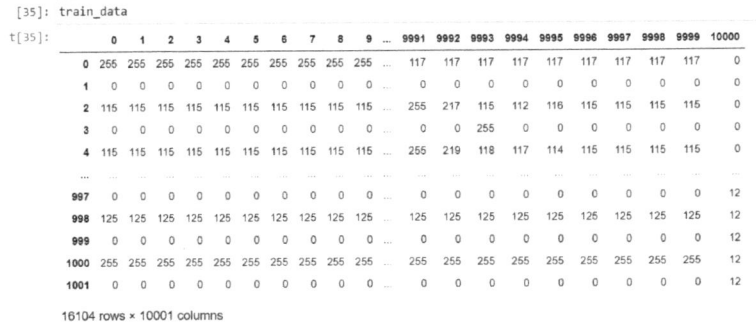

```
[35]: train_data
```

	0	1	2	3	4	5	6	7	8	9	...	9991	9992	9993	9994	9995	9996	9997	9998	9999	10000
0	255	255	255	255	255	255	255	255	255	255	...	117	117	117	117	117	117	117	117	117	0
1	0	0	0	0	0	0	0	0	0	0	...	0	0	0	0	0	0	0	0	0	0
2	115	115	115	115	115	115	115	115	115	115	...	255	217	115	112	116	115	115	115	115	0
3	0	0	0	0	0	0	0	0	0	0	...	0	0	255	0	0	0	0	0	0	0
4	115	115	115	115	115	115	115	115	115	115	...	255	219	118	117	114	115	115	115	115	0
...																					
997	0	0	0	0	0	0	0	0	0	0	...	0	0	0	0	0	0	0	0	0	12
998	125	125	125	125	125	125	125	125	125	125	...	125	125	125	125	125	125	125	125	125	12
999	0	0	0	0	0	0	0	0	0	0	...	0	0	0	0	0	0	0	0	0	12
1000	255	255	255	255	255	255	255	255	255	255	...	255	255	255	255	255	255	255	255	255	12
1001	0	0	0	0	0	0	0	0	0	0	...	0	0	0	0	0	0	0	0	0	12

16104 rows × 10001 columns

Figure 1.30 The primary data frame

6. Now these data frames exist as variable data structures in the main memory, as soon as the python kernel is turned off or restarted all these data frames will be lost. So the primary data frame is saved on the hard drive as a CSV(comma separated value

file) file.

```
train_data.to_csv(r'C:\Users\91989\Documents\1FINAL PROJECT\hundred dimensions\product_data.csv',index = False)
```

Figure 1.31 Saving data frame as .csv file

1.10 Training the model

10.1.1 Preparing the data for training

1. The primary data frame was saved as a .csv file at the end of chapter 2, this can be reopened in Pandas data frame with it's pixel values and their corresponding labels.

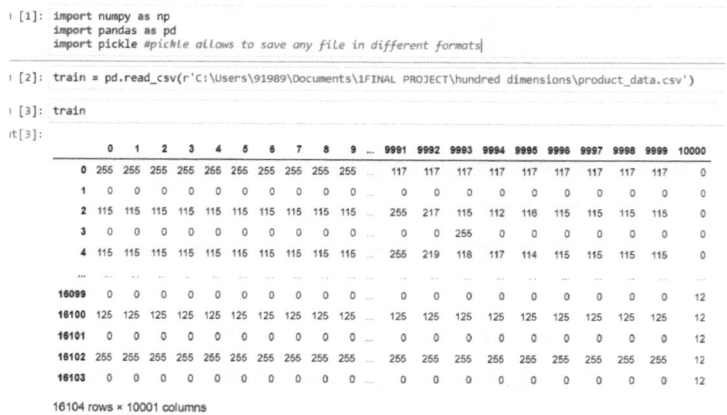

Figure 1.32 Primary data frame

2. The very first step in training the CNN model is to isolate labels of every image as it is an independent input, the value that is to be predicted for future examples based on these images.

```
labels = train1[['10000']]
train1.drop(train1.columns[[10000]],axis=1,inplace=True)
train1.head()
```

	0	1	2	3	4	5	6	7	8	9	...	9990	9991	9992	9993	9994	9995	9996	9997	9998	9999
0	255	255	255	255	255	255	255	255	255	255	...	117	117	117	117	117	117	117	117	117	117
1	0	0	0	0	0	0	0	0	0	0	...	0	0	0	0	0	0	0	0	0	0
2	115	115	115	115	115	115	115	115	115	115	...	255	255	217	115	112	116	115	115	115	115
3	0	0	0	0	0	0	0	0	0	0	...	0	0	0	255	0	0	0	0	0	0
4	115	115	115	115	115	115	115	115	115	115	...	255	255	219	118	117	114	115	115	115	115

5 rows × 10000 columns

Figure 1.33 Labels extracted

```
5]: labels
5]:
```

	10000
0	0
1	0
2	0
3	0
4	0
...	
16099	12
16100	12
16101	12
16102	12
16103	12

Figure 1.34 Labels

3. Now, these label values cannot be directly fed as an input or the value to be mapped by the convolutional neural network because label values in form of whole number 0…12 cannot be recognized directly instead these must be labeled with 0s and 1s. Suppose for entire data set, the label '0' is for Cadbury silk then label for every image in the data set of cadbury silk shall be '1' while rest of the labels are '0' i.e **they are not even considered. This step is known as classes to categorical.**

```
labels=np.array(labels)

from keras.utils.np_utils import to_categorical
cat=to_categorical(labels,num_classes=13)

cat

array([[1., 0., 0., ..., 0., 0., 0.],
       [1., 0., 0., ..., 0., 0., 0.],
       [1., 0., 0., ..., 0., 0., 0.],
       ...,
       [0., 0., 0., ..., 0., 0., 1.],
       [0., 0., 0., ..., 0., 0., 1.],
       [0., 0., 0., ..., 0., 0., 1.]], dtype=float32)
```

Figure 1.35

4. Final step before training the model will be modifying the dimension of the input image data frame by converting all the image values to a **numpy array (CNN input must be a numpy array)** of dimensions **100x100x1** because the image dimensions are 100x100 of single channel therefore the additional 1.

```
[11]: l=[]
      for i in range(16104):
          l.append(np.array(train1[i:i+1]).reshape(100,100,1))
```

Figure 1.36

1.11 The CNN Model

1. Importing necessary libraries to design a custom CNN architecture

```
import keras
from keras.models import Model
from keras.layers import *
from keras import optimizers
from keras.layers import Input, Dense
from keras.models import Sequential
from keras.layers import Dense
from keras.layers import Dropout
from keras.layers import Flatten
from keras.layers.convolutional import Conv2D
from keras.layers.convolutional import MaxPooling2D
from keras.utils import np_utils
```

Figure 1.37 CNN model libraries

2. Defining the architecture of the model

```
model = Sequential()
model.add(Conv2D(30, (5, 5), input_shape=(100,100,1), activation='relu'))
model.add(MaxPooling2D(pool_size=(2, 2)))
model.add(Conv2D(15, (3, 3), activation='relu'))
model.add(MaxPooling2D(pool_size=(2, 2)))
model.add(Dropout(0.2))
model.add(Flatten())
model.add(Dense(128, activation='relu'))
model.add(Dense(50, activation='relu'))
model.add(Dense(13, activation='softmax'))
# Compile model
model.compile(loss='categorical_crossentropy', optimizer='adam', metrics=['accuracy'])
```

Figure 1.38 The CNN

- **Defining the terms used in the model**

1. **Sequential ():** This method allows to create a customized CNN architecture by letting the user to stack new layers one after the another in the model. As a result the subsequent layers are added in the model.

19

2. **Model.add():** Because the very first statement in the code was **Sequential()**, model.add() allows the user to add new layers to the model and expand the architecture of the model.

a) **Conv2D (30, (5,5)):** It is the number of kernels present in the first layer that implement the filter process of the first layer on the input data i.e the pixel matrix.

b) **Input_shape (100,100,1):** Here this argument defines the number of neurons required to take the input of 100x100 dimension image which is 10000 neurons in the input layer.

c) **Activation='relu':** Here the rectified linear units are the hypothesis function in which the result is predicted and converted into terms of 0 and max value to ease the mathematical computation.

3. **MaxPooling2d (pool_size= (2,2)):** Here a hidden layer that performs pooling operation is added to extract important features from the feature map. A kernel of size (2,2) that performs pooling operation is defined.

4. **Model.add(dropout (0.2)):** This method drops the results of random neurons in the architecture to compensate for regularization (concept of over-fitting and under-fitting).

5. **Model.add(Dense(128, activation='relu')) :**
a) **Model.add(Dense)** - Here this argument adds a full connected layer where each and every neuron is connected with its previous layer to feed forward the output predicted values to the output layer. The input neurons in this layer are 128 and activation function to feed forward the values to the next layer is Relu.

6. **Model.add(dense(13, activation='softmax'))**- This the output layer, this layer is too a fully connected layer where all neurons are connected with each other. **Softmax returns the highest value among the vector containing the probabilities for each class.**

7. **Model.compile(loss='categorical crossentropy', optimizer ='adam', metric = ['accuracy'])** – here this command compiles this model with categorical crossentropy determines the loss of the model and adjusts the weights and bias appropriately.ow executing the model, with epoch = 50 (it runs through the entire data set 50 times during training) and batch_size = 16, at a time 16 examples are taken in every iteration.

```
model.fit(np.array(1), cat, epochs=50, batch_size=32,shuffle=True,verbose=1)
```

Figure 1.39

8. Model trained results

```
Epoch 47/50
1007/1007 [==============================] - 109s 108ms/step - loss: 0.0890
- accuracy: 0.9798
Epoch 48/50
1007/1007 [==============================] - 109s 108ms/step - loss: 0.0779
- accuracy: 0.9808
Epoch 49/50
1007/1007 [==============================] - 109s 109ms/step - loss: 0.0899
- accuracy: 0.9799
Epoch 50/50
1007/1007 [==============================] - 108s 108ms/step - loss: 0.0791
- accuracy: 0.9827
```

Figure 1.40 Trained model

Here the model is trained with 98.27 % accuracy using 50 epochs. Here **epoch stands for number of iterations the model goes through the dataset.**

- The trained model must be stored in the hard drive so that it can deployed independently without training it over again. Also saving a model after it is trained is an efficient computationally.

- These saved weights can be deployed on a SBC such as raspberry pi.

```
in [13].
from keras.models import model_from_json
```

Figure 1.41 Library to save model weights

```
model_json = model.to_json()
with open(r'C:\Users\91989\Documents\1FINAL PROJ
    json_file.write(model_json)
# serialize weights to HDF5
model.save_weights(r'C:\Users\91989\Documents\1F
```

Figure 1.42 Saving the weights as HDF5 file and model architecture as JSON

21

1.12   Trained model output

```python
def CNN_test(image):
    train = []
    img = cv2.imread(image,cv2.IMREAD_GRAYSCALE)
    dim = (100,100)
    img = cv2.resize(img,dim)
    img=np.reshape(img,[1,100,100,1])
    train.append(img)
    result=loaded_model.predict_classes(img)
    if(result == [0]):
        print("Cadbury Silk")
        image = cv2.imread(r'C:\Users\91989\Documents\1FINAL PROJECT\train\Validation\cadbu
        plt.imshow(image)
    if(result == [1]):
        print("Coca cola; cold drink")
        image = cv2.imread(r'C:\Users\91989\Documents\1FINAL PROJECT\train\Validation\cocac
        plt.imshow(image)
    if(result == [2]):
        print("Fanta")
        image = cv2.imread(r'C:\Users\91989\Documents\1FINAL PROJECT\train\Validation\fanta
        plt.imshow(image)
    if(result == [4]):
        print("Kitkat")
        image = cv2.imread(r'C:\Users\91989\Documents\1FINAL PROJECT\train\Validation\kitka
        plt.imshow(image)
    if(result == [3]):
        print("Five Star")
        image = cv2.imread(r'C:\Users\91989\Documents\1FINAL PROJECT\train\Validation\five_
        plt.imshow(image)
    if(result == [5]):
        print("kurkure green")
        image = cv2.imread(r'C:\Users\91989\Documents\1FINAL PROJECT\train\Validation\green
```

Figure 1.43 Trained model implementation

- Here a method CNN test is defined which takes an image location as an argument and performs multiple important steps listed as below:

1. The image is read via **opencv's cv2.imread()** which enables us to read images from directories in different formats i.e images can be converted to different formats while it's being read from the directories like cv2.IMREAD_GRAYSCALE

2. The image read into user variable img is then resized to the dimensions according to the dimension of input layer of CNN by **cv2.resize()**

3. **Input to Convolutional Neural Networks is always in numpy array format** so the input image is converted to numpy array of single dimension and of single channel grey scale.

1.13   Output

• Input image is

Figure 1.44 Input image

```
: image = cv2.imread(r'C:\Users\91989\Documents\1FINAL PROJECT\test images\silk1.jpg',cv2.IMREAD_GRAYSCALE)
```
```
: CNN_test(image)
```
```
WARNING:tensorflow:From <ipython-input-3-0370610b7420>:13: Sequential.predict_classes (from tensorflow.python.
ential) is deprecated and will be removed after 2021-01-01.
Instructions for updating:
Please use instead:* `np.argmax(model.predict(x), axis=-1)`,   if your model does multi-class classification
a `softmax` last-layer activation).* `(model.predict(x) > 0.5).astype("int32")`,   if your model does binary c
(e.g. if it uses a `sigmoid` last-layer activation).
Cadbury Silk
0
```
Figure 1.45 Input image result

1.14   Hardware flow diagram

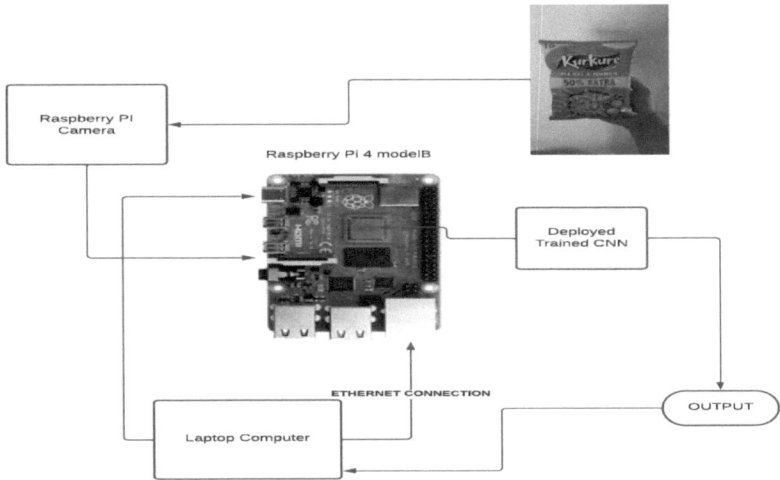

1.15   Raspberry Pi
1.15.1   Raspberry pi 4 mode B 4GB

- Raspberry pi is a **single board computer** developed by the raspberry foundation and released in 2012. This release of this device revolutionized IoT applications and application of machine learning algorithms in devices with low computation power.

- Raspberry pi runs on Linux based bullseye operating systems such as debian although OS such as windows can be made to run.

- In this project raspberry pi 4 4GB model B with 64 bit Broadcom BCM2711 quad-core cortex-A-72 (ARM V8) SoC @ 1.5GHz.

- Through MicroSD OS is booted and operations are performed.

Figure 1.46 Raspberry PI 4 model B

1.16 Raspberry Pi setup

Figure 1.47 Raspberry Pi setup

- Raspberry Pi camera requires no additional installation, simply plug it in and capture the image with the command **libcamera-jpeg –o image.jpg.**
- The above command captures and stores image in whichever directory user executes the command from.

1.17 Raspberry PI output

Figure 1.48 Raspberry PI input image

```
pi@raspberrypi:~ $ cd final_project
pi@raspberrypi:~/final_project $ ls
attempt.py          final_model_json.h5     __pycache__     testimage
final_model.json    lays3.jpg               silk.jpg        test_images
pi@raspberrypi:~/final_project $ python3 attempt.py
Jai Swaminarayan
0
Cadbury silk
```

Figure 1.49 OUTPUT

1.18 Test results merits and demerits

- The trained model accurately predicts certain images but suffers from adversarial problem such as images of common color such as Lays green and Green kurkure are often inaccurately predicted.

- Image captured at a certain distance are inaccurately predicted so a thorough data set needs to be created with a more varied image orientation.

- Image captured at some distance often results into inaccurate prediction.

- Model works perfectly well for objects placed at a distance of 15 to 17 cm.

- As CNN model is trained in pc, it's weights can be deployed in the SBCs and can be executed independently using python environment due to python interpreters

.

26

1.19 Conclusion & future enhancements

This project has been developed as a prototype to an idea that a device can automate "hold-observe-purchase" experience by utilizing a pre-trained image recognition algorithm (trained on computer) which helps in generating a transactional ledger and then deployed on a SBC. In order to train a deep learning model it requires a large volume of image data set which was created from custom images acquired from internet as well as captured using cameras in mobile phones to serve as the training volume.Using this trained model, images are recognized and it's transactional ledger is generated as subsequent products are fed as an input using a camera attached to the SBC.

Raspberry Pi being a SBC, this device is connected to a centralized server which helps in maintaining a database of price and discount of different retail products. Also a user database can be maintained in the server which can be retrieved when a user uses a magnetic strip card provided by the retail market firm to track points and rewards to log into his/her account via a magnetic card reader attached to the raspberry pi.

With these details readily available at hand, as user starts adding products to the cart and the device recognizing it, the transactional ledger is generated and at the end the data from the raspberry pi node is shared with the central server which is then shared with the user via app (paytm, etc) or text message.

REFERENCES

[1] Tonioni, Alessio & Serra, Eugenio & Di Stefano, Luigi. (2018). A deep learning pipeline for product recognition on store shelves. 25-31. 10.1109/IPAS.2018.8708890.

[2] http://lup.lub.lu.se/student-papers/record/8985308 "AI Based Machine-Vision for retail self-checkout system"

[3] Reuben Pinto and Aisha Fernandes, (2021)IoT based quick retail checkout using machine learning and rfid technology JETIR August 2021, Volume 8, Issue 8 "

[4] F. Femling, A. Olsson and F. Alonso-Fernandez, "Fruit and Vegetable Identification Using Machine Learning for Retail Applications," *2018 14th International Conference on Signal-Image Technology & Internet-Based Systems (SITIS)*, 2018, pp. 9-15, doi: 10.1109/SITIS.2018.00013

[5] Y. Lecun, Y. Bengio, and G. Hinton, "Deep learning," Nature, vol. 521, no. 7553, pp. 436–444, 5 2015

YOUR KNOWLEDGE HAS VALUE